November Journal Jumpstarts

A Month of Creative Writing Prompts

Written by
Cindy Barden

Editors: Barbara G. Hoffman and Michael Batty

Cover and Interior Design: Good Neighbor Press, Inc.

Illustrator: Chris Nye

FS112132 November Journal Jumpstarts

All rights reserved—Printed in the U.S.A.
23740 Hawthorne Boulevard
Torrance, CA 90505-5927

Notice! Pages may be reproduced for classroom or home use only, not for commercial resale. No part of this publication may be reproduced for storage in a retrieval system or transmitted in any form or by any means—electronic, mechanical, recording, etc.—without the prior permission of the publisher. Reproduction of these materials for an entire school or school system is strictly prohibited.

Copyright © 2000 Frank Schaffer Publications, Inc.

Table of Contents

November

© Frank Schaffer Publications, Inc.

Introduction

An empty journal is filled with infinite possibilities.

Writing regularly in a journal helps us to develop our imaginations, encourages us to express our thoughts, feelings, and dreams, and provides a way to communicate experiences in words and pictures. Many students feel frustrated when asked to keep a journal. They may not be sure of what to write, or they may be intimidated by a blank sheet of paper. Even professional writers occasionally face "writer's block." The Journal Jumpstarts series provides ideas and suggestions for daily journal entries. Each book contains 29 jumpstarts. You could give each student a photocopy of the same page or provide a variety of pages and allow students to choose their own topics. You may have students who will be able to sit and write without jumpstarts. At times students may prefer to express their thoughts through drawings or with a combination of drawings and writing. Be encouraging!

Through making regular entries in journals, students become more observant of themselves and the world around them. Journal writing on a regular basis strengthens students' attention spans and abilities to focus. Keeping journals promotes self-esteem because students are doing something for themselves—not for grades or in competition with others. A journal can become an essential friend, a confidante in times of personal crisis.

Encourage students to get into the journal habit by setting aside writing time every day at about the same time, such as first thing in the morning or shortly before lunch. Share their journal time by writing in your own journal. What better way to encourage a good habit than by example!

Note: Assure students that what they write is confidential. Provide a safe, secure place for students to store their journals. Respect their privacy, as you would expect your privacy to be respected—read their journals by invitation only.

© Frank Schaffer Publications, Inc.

Name _____ Date _____

Time Alone

Write about your favorite place to spend
time alone. When do you like to go
there? What do you like about it?

_____

_____

_____

_____

_____

_____

_____

_____

_____

_____

_____

_____

_____

_____

_____

_____

_____

Name _____ Date _____

Friday Favorites

Write about Fridays at school or at home.
What do you like most about Fridays?
What do you like least?

_____

_____

_____

_____

_____

_____

_____

_____

_____

_____

_____

_____

_____

_____

_____

_____

_____

_____

_____

_____

© Frank Schaffer Publications, Inc.

Getting Along

Write about things that you do to get
along with the people in your family.

_____

_____

_____

_____

_____

_____

_____

_____

_____

_____

_____

_____

_____

_____

_____

_____

Name *Zehra*   Date _____

Old Friends

Write about the oldest person that you know
with whom you enjoy spending time.
Describe what you enjoy doing with
him or her and explain why.

Sara was my
best friend,
we did everything
together. She even went
to the same Sunday
school I did! When I
left the school we were
very sad. :(. But I saw
her atleast once after
a year. :)

Name _____ Date _____

School Spirit

What is school spirit? Do you have school spirit?
Write about why or why not.

_____

_____

_____

_____

_____

_____

_____

_____

_____

_____

_____

_____

_____

_____

_____

Name _____   Date _____

Listen to Me

Is there a special person to whom you go when you really need to talk about a problem? Explain why you feel comfortable talking to him or her.

_____

_____

_____

_____

_____

_____

_____

_____

_____

_____

_____

_____

_____

_____

_____

_____

_____

© Frank Schaffer Publications, Inc.

Name _____ Date _____

Girls or Boys Only

Are there sports that only girls should play and sports that only boys should play? Write about your opinion.

_____

_____

_____

_____

_____

_____

_____

_____

_____

_____

_____

_____

_____

_____

_____

Teamwork

A "team player" works with others to complete a group project. Are you a team player at home or at school? If so, give examples. If not, describe why you aren't.

_____

_____

_____

_____

_____

_____

_____

_____

_____

                         _____

                         _____

                         _____

                         _____

                         _____

                         _____

                         _____

Musical Marvel

Do you know how to play a musical instrument?
If you do, describe how you felt about learning to
play it. If not, write about an instrument that
you'd like to play and explain why.

_____

_____

_____

_____

_____

_____

_____

_____

_____

_____

_____

_____

_____

_____

_____

_____

Novembery

In some parts of the country,
November is a damp, cold month.
People sometimes say they feel
"Novembery." Explain what you
think they mean. Do you ever
feel Novembery?

_____

_____

_____

_____

_____

_____

_____

_____

_____

_____

_____

_____

_____

_____

_____

_____

_____

_____

_____

© Frank Schaffer Publications, Inc.

Name _____ Date _____

Shy

Have you ever met someone new or gone to a new place and not known what to say or do? Describe what you did when that happened to you or what you could do to help someone who is shy and new to your school.

_____

_____

_____

_____

_____

_____

_____

_____

_____

_____

_____

_____

_____

_____

_____

Name _____   Date _____

V.I.G.

Pretend that you've invited a very important guest to dinner tomorrow. Who is the guest? What foods will you serve? Why did you choose those foods?

_____

_____

_____

_____

_____

_____

_____

_____

_____

_____

_____

_____

_____

_____

_____

_____

_____

© Frank Schaffer Publications, Inc.

Name _____ Date _____

Favorite Movie

Write about your all-time favorite movie.
Why did you like it? Why would other
people like it?

_____

_____

_____

_____

_____

_____

_____

_____

_____

_____

_____

_____

_____

_____

_____

Name _____ Date _____

Strange Candy

Write about the strangest flavor of candy that you have ever tasted. You may describe a real candy or make one up.

_____

_____

_____

_____

_____

_____

_____

_____

_____

_____

_____

_____

_____

_____

_____

Name _____ Date _____

Animal Power

Fish can swim, birds can fly, and monkeys can swing through the trees. Write about something that an animal can do that you wish you could, too. Pick any animal that you like.

_____

_____

_____

_____

_____

_____

_____

_____

_____

_____

_____

_____

_____

_____

_____

_____

Name _____   Date _____

Best Vacation

Have you ever gone on vacation?
If so, describe the best vacation
you've ever had. If not, describe
where you would like to go
and what you would like to do
on vacation.

Once I went on vacation
to Florida. I went becaus all my uncles, Aunts and cousins

_____

_____

_____

_____

_____

_____

_____

_____

_____

_____

_____

_____

17
reproducible

© Frank Schaffer Publications, Inc.

Name _____ Date _____

Making Friends

Write about a friend of yours. How did you become friends with him or her?
Did you like to do the same kinds of things? What were the things that made
you friends?

_____

_____

_____

_____

_____

_____

_____

_____

_____

_____

_____

_____

_____

_____

_____

_____

_____

Name _____ Date _____

Great Hits

What is your favorite song? Write about your favorite song, why you like it, and what it's about. Describe where you were when you heard the song for the first time.

_____

_____

_____

_____

_____

_____

_____

_____

_____

_____

_____

_____

_____

_____

_____

_____

_____

© Frank Schaffer Publications, Inc.

An Audience

Describe how you feel about talking, singing,
playing an instrument, or dancing in front of
an audience. Do you feel comfortable?
Why or why not?

_____

_____

_____

_____

_____

_____

_____

_____

_____

_____

_____

_____

_____

_____

_____

_____

Name _____ Date _____

Patriotism

Patriotism means showing love for your country.
What do you do to show love for your country?

_____

_____

_____

_____

_____

_____

_____

_____

_____

_____

_____

_____

_____

_____

_____

© Frank Schaffer Publications, Inc.

Name _____ Date _____

Lion Tamer

If you had the chance to be an
assistant lion tamer and to learn the
job from the best lion tamer in the
world, would you take it? Why or
why not?

_____

_____

_____

_____

_____

_____

_____

_____

_____

_____

_____

_____

_____

_____

_____

_____

Name _____   Date _____

About Me

Describe something about yourself that stands out. It could be a feature, like your hair, or a skill, like jumping rope. If you wish, make something up.

_____
_____
_____
_____
_____
_____
_____
_____
_____
_____
_____
_____
_____
_____
_____
_____

© Frank Schaffer Publications, Inc.

Orange and Yellow Day

If today were Orange and Yellow Day and you could only eat foods that were orange and yellow, what would you have for breakfast, lunch, and supper?

MENU

_____

_____

_____

_____

_____

_____

_____

_____

_____

_____

_____

_____

_____

_____

_____

_____

_____

Machine for a Day

If you could be a kind of machine, which kind would you like to be? Describe what you think it would be like to be that kind of machine.

_____

_____

_____

_____

_____

_____

_____

_____

_____

_____

_____

_____

_____

_____

_____

_____

_____

_____

© Frank Schaffer Publications, Inc.

Name _____   Date _____

Turkey Talk

Imagine that you are a Pilgrim boy or girl writing a letter to a friend you left in England who has never seen a turkey. Describe a turkey to him or her.

_____

_____

_____

_____

_____

_____

_____

_____

_____

_____

_____

_____

_____

_____

_____

_____

Giving Thanks

Thanksgiving is a day to celebrate many good things that we have in our lives. Write about three things that you are thankful for and describe why.

_____

_____

_____

_____

_____

_____

_____

_____

_____

_____

_____

_____

_____

_____

_____

_____

_____

© Frank Schaffer Publications, Inc.

If You Were a Pilgrim

Imagine being a Pilgrim, journeying to a distant new land across a vast ocean. From the point of view of a Pilgrim, write about how you would have felt when you first landed in the strange New World.

_____

_____

_____

_____

_____

_____

_____

_____

_____

_____

                        _____

                        _____

                        _____

                        _____

                        _____

                        _____

                        _____

Alien Visitors

Aliens from outer space have landed in your backyard. Before reporters and officials arrive, you have time to ask three questions. Write the three questions that you would most like to have answered by beings from outer space. Then write how they might respond.

_____

_____

_____

_____

_____

_____

_____

_____

_____

_____

_____

_____

_____

_____

_____

_____

© Frank Schaffer Publications, Inc.

Name _____ Date _____

Rationing

Write about how you would feel if something that you really liked to eat or drink was suddenly available only on a very limited basis (like soda once a month, hamburgers once every two months, or pie once a year).

_____

_____

_____

_____

_____

_____

_____

_____

_____

_____

_____

_____

_____

_____

_____

_____